Positivity on Purpose

Intentionally Create More Wealth, Happiness and Abundance

By Nicole Bandes

ISBN-13:
978-0615471532

ISBN-10:
0615471536

DEDICATION

For my husband, Jeff, who supported me in the writing of this book.
And for my son, TJ, who is as big a cheerleader as they come.

CONTENTS

ACKNOWLEDGMENTS

I would first like to thank my 6th grade teacher. He was the first person to instill in me a love of writing. I have known since then that I was meant to write a book someday.

I would also like to thank my mom. She gave me the love of reading. Although I've never been a fast reader, her love inspired me to stick with it no matter what.

Thank you to each of my coaching clients for continuing to provide me with excellent illustrations that will help many others to grow as well.

DISCLAIMER

Please note that the information within this book may not be appropriate for everyone. There are some instances where the guidance of a qualified therapist or other mental health provider may be necessary.

While the author does not believe any of the suggestions in this book will bring harm in any way, it is up to the reader to make their own determinations as to whether the advice is suitable for them at this point in time. If the reader is unable to make this determination, it is suggested that they seek professional guidance.

INTRODUCTION

You have many choices in the books you read. In fact, there are over 160,000 new books published every year. Thank you for taking the time to read mine. I truly wish for you what I have been able to acquire for myself: a positive mental attitude.

I wasn't always a positive person. In fact, quite the opposite is true. I grew up in a home where my dad was regularly unemployed and my mom did her best to support the family on one income. I often went to school with high water pants (where were Capri pants when I needed them!) and occasionally had to take advantage of reduced cost school lunches.

My parents weren't into personal development and didn't really have goals outside of making sure to have food on the table through the end of the week. Why would they, no one taught them either. Self esteem was not a skill I was taught at all. In fact, I learned how not to feel good about who I was. I spent most of my teen and college years depressed and even took Prozac for a few years. Fortunately, I had an interest in understanding why my family and I were the way we were and what we might be able to do to get "fixed".

I began to explore more about psychology and began to learn about myself. It was all quite fascinating and I learned a lot about human nature in general. With all this study, the university honored me with a degree in Psychology. However, I wasn't instantly "fixed". I was still confused and looking for answers. Unfortunately, there was a very large piece of the puzzle missing.

After college, I found myself working in various jobs. None of them really felt quite right. I knew I always felt best when I could impart what I had learned on others and help to motivate and encourage them. However, I couldn't yet see how I could make a full time career out of that. Also, I didn't feel like I should be helping others when I was still struggling myself. I had too often heard the phrase, "those that can't do, teach" and I didn't want that to be me.

During the years after college, I started several different network marketing companies. I had moderate success with a few of them but nothing stellar. I never walked across any stages. One of the things I truly love about network marketing and direct sales businesses is that they encourage you to explore as much personal development as possible. That's just what I did but most of it was sporadic and inconsistent.

About a decade after college, I really began to invest in myself. I took classes, read books and attended seminars on personal development. I kept hearing the same things over and over, but knew that eventually there would be something that lit the fuse and would change my life forever. At least that's what I thought then.

As I look back on the before and after, I can't really attribute my personal breakthrough to one given moment. Rather, it was a series of changes in my life that occurred all within a short period of time. Many of these changes are what I now base my work on as a coach and speaker. Of course it is also what I base my writing on. You will read about some of them in these pages.

Once upon a time, people told me I was always a happy and positive person. Deep down inside, I knew that was an act. I shied away from those compliments feeling like a fake. Now I glow with pride and excitement when someone recognizes the hard work I have put in to become the happy and positive person I am today. I hope that I can share some of that with you and maybe, just maybe, a little bit of it will rub off.

HOW TO USE THIS BOOK

"When life gives you lemons, make lemonade."

"The grass is always greener on the other side."

"It's always darkest before the dawn."

"Every cloud has a silver lining."

It seems there are a million little motivational phrases meant to cheer us up when things aren't going well. Of course, the last thing we usually want at that point in time is for someone all happy-go-lucky to come rain on our pity party parade. It could be that the only thing we really want to do is have someone tell us how right we are to be miserable and commiserate along with us.

Just how positive are you really though? Let's find out.

The Quiz

Answer the following questions truthfully and with your first guess. Circle the number that best fits.

1= Poor 2 = Average 3 = Good 4 = EXCELLENT

1. I can see the benefit to most situations.

1   2   3   4

2. I surround myself with positive people.

1   2   3   4

3. I do not blame other people for my current situation.

1   2   3   4

4. I do not blame current circumstances for my present situation.

1   2   3   4

5. I tend to see the silver lining easily.

1   2   3   4

6. I am able to help others see things more positively.

1   2   3   4

7. People tell me I'm always happy.

1   2   3   4

8. I seem to be lucky.

1   2   3   4

9. I easily adapt to change.

1   2   3   4

10. I easily bounce back from negative events.

1   2   3   4

Score your results:

0-10 = You have a lot of work to go. If you are ready to take on the challenge and truly want a more positive life, then you only have up to go from here! The first step is to WANT it.

11-20 = Positivity is a struggle but you manage to be happy occassionally. With some effort, you can increase your natural positive attitude.

21-30 = You are on the right track. It takes a lot to bring you down. Keep up the efforts and adding to your tool box can help keep you up even more often!

31-37 = A little fine tuning never hurt. Keep reading for some good refreshers and tips to keep your mind focused and positivity flowing.

38-40 = You are at the TOP of your game. Thank you for reviewing this book before handing it to a friend. It's always good to know what you are recommending.

So how do you gain a positive attitude after being the miserable oh-woe-is-me character who has more to gain from being negative than from making the effort to seek a more positive attitude?

This book is intended to be a step-by-step guide to creating a permanent positive attitude. Through taking conscious action steps to challenge and change your negative thoughts, you can tap into the subconscious mind to create lasting change. It will take practice and effort, but with time, the techniques shared in these pages will become natural. It won't always be easy but it will always be worth it.

I kept this book short because it is my belief that a short book that gets read is more effective than a long, highly detailed book that doesn't get read. The principles have worked well for me as well as for those I have worked with in my own coaching practice. The benefit to you is that it won't take you long to get through it and you can pick it up at any time, flip to any chapter and begin working on changing your current negative attitude.

The chapters follow a certain flow but do not feel like you must do them in the order I have selected for you. Choose which chapters seem to feel right at any given time and start there.

Once you have selected a chapter, learn the principles and work to incorporate them into your daily life. Don't wait till the proverbial poo hits the fan because it is often far more difficult to pull yourself out of a negative attitude when it is at its worst. Use the techniques on daily challenges such as rush hour traffic, screaming kids, angry bosses and irate customers. But, do not attempt to start using any of the techniques when all of these challenges happen at once. You will certainly be overwhelmed and decide this book just doesn't work. That's like taking a baby aspirin in the middle of a heart attack. Good luck with that.

Most chapters will include an action step. This is a step or process you can begin to incorporate into your life immediately. The faster you introduce these steps and the more frequently you use them, the more you will get from this book.

Some chapters will also include a REAL WORLD example. These examples are meant to help you see how this process has worked for others. Their situations may not be the same as yours but may give you a little insight and provide some illustration. Use the examples to see how the process may fit into your own life. Of course, the names marked with a * are changed to protect the client's privacy.

Most of all, take your time and enjoy the process. Keep an eye on how you are doing and begin to notice how you start to automatically shift thoughts that may have once been negative into positive ones. The more you practice, the more natural it becomes.

1

THE IMPORTANCE OF BEING POSITIVE

"Attitude is a little thing that makes a big difference."
- Winston Churchill

There is power in the positive attitude. That's why so many personal development gurus, coaches, speakers and trainers highly recommend it. When you are struggling to maintain a positive attitude it can often become frustrating to continually hear that a positive attitude is the key to what you most want in life. Maintaining a positive attitude requires a lot of ongoing effort but the rewards are tremendous.

Control

Being positive allows you to remain in control giving you the option to make a change. Being negative removes the control and makes you a victim without power. It's unfortunately all too common to stay so focused on the negative aspects of our lives that change becomes almost impossible. By making a shift in our attitude, we can free up our minds to focus on opportunities to make things better. This leads us to our next benefit.

Opportunities

Being positive means looking for opportunities. A negative attitude closes you off to the opportunities. You might be so focused on what is WRONG that you miss the chance to have something RIGHT. When you think to yourself, "Nothing good ever happens to me," then even when something good comes along, you dismiss it as "too good" to be true. The statement becomes a self-fulfilling prophecy.

Learning valuable lessons

Having a positive attitude allows you to find the valuable lessons in even the most negative of situations. Being negative prevents you from learning and growing based on the experiences that are happening to you now.

Being positive allows you to learn from the mistakes and failures of yourself and others. Being negative turns fail into a four letter word. Failure is an opportunity to learn and grow. However, if you look at failure with a negative mindset, then it is just one more stab to the self-esteem, one more validation that you aren't good enough, smart enough, or just aren't enough. Embracing failure with a positive attitude allows you to use the experience to transform who you are and what you do.

Get physical

A positive attitude is good for the physical body. It keeps us healthy and helps us to recover quickly. It increases our energy and vitality. It even makes us stronger! Applied Kinesiology is a form of muscle testing where strength is used to determine how good or bad something is for the physical body. To see the actual process in action and learn how to try this for yourself, go to:

http://goldeneaglescoaching.com/beliefs/positive-thinkings-effects-on-your-body/.

In this video there is a demonstration on how positive statements can make a person physically stronger while negative statements make them physically weaker. I encourage you to try this for yourself.

To relate to this on another level, we frequently hear about the benefits of prayer on those with serious or terminal illness: When the individual prays or has a significant positive outlook for their future, their long term prognosis is far better than those with a negative outlook. This is the power of positive thought on the physical body.

Now that you know why it is in your best interest to think positively, let's explore how to do it without resorting to the "fake it till you make it" learning curve.

2

DO I ALWAYS HAVE TO BE POSITIVE?

"It's so hard when I have to, and so easy when I want to."
- Annie Gottlier

All the quotes and sayings, books and seminars, self-help gurus and experts preach to us that we have to be positive all the time. They tell us that being positive is the best, fastest way to get what it is we most desire. But this is the real world. Is it really possible to be positive ALL the time?

The answer is no. There is not a single person on this planet that is able to maintain a positive thought process or outlook all the time. Not one. Everyone from Anthony

Robbins and Oprah Winfrey to the Pope feel negative emotions from time to time. Life happens. We all experience various situations in our life that will influence our feelings and emotions, sometimes for the good and sometimes for the not-so-good. It is impossible to not at least momentarily have a lapse in our positive attitude when something bad happens.

REAL WORLD

Lynn* was a life coach who had been through some extremely traumatic experiences during her life. Lynn's husband had abused her physically and emotionally for many years until she was finally able to get out of that horrible situation. Lynn chose to be a life coach primarily to help other women that were experiencing similar situations to know that they, too, could make it out and be okay.

While it would seem that Lynn should be able to handle any situation after that kind of experience, she still struggled with much of her own personal challenges. She found it difficult to surmount many of these challenges; things that she couldn't find a single positive aspect to and, therefore, continued to feel her negative emotions and allow them to affect her attitude which naturally hurt her business.

I introduced Lynn to many of the concepts included in this book. At first, she resisted and didn't feel that any of it was worth it. It took some time, but with practice, she was able to reduce her negative attitude from lasting months down to just a day or two at a time. And with a more positive attitude, she was able to attract more clients and be the role model they needed her to be.

It is okay to feel negative emotions. In fact, it may be incredibly unhealthy NOT to allow those negative feelings out once in a while. The key is to not allow those moments of depression, anger or frustration to overtake our lives.

Far too many individuals will get so wrapped up in the feelings that they cease to progress forward. The negative thoughts then begin to attract more negative feelings or thoughts creating a vicious cycle downward. It's a trap that is hard to get out of.

ACTION STEP

The next time a negative emotion comes up, allow yourself to feel the feeling fully and completely. If you normally feel the emotion for a week before getting over it, work to bring that down to a day and then to an hour. Eventually you will learn to reduce the overall time you experience an emotion to less than 15 minutes before you can recover and get back to the emotions and feelings that best serve you.

EXTRA CREDIT

To take this process a step further, begin to record in a journal the negative emotions and how long they last. If you are really analytical, you can even create a graph of the progress you are making. Don't get too wrapped up in it though: This is just a quick visual for you to understand and celebrate your progress.

Remember, it takes practice.

"Optimist: A man who is chased up a tree by a lion but enjoys the scenery anyway."
- Walter Winchell

3

POSITIVE THINKING IS A HABIT

"We are what we repeatedly do.
Excellence then, is not an act, but a habit."
–Aristotle

It is a rare individual that comes out of the womb thinking positively almost all of the time. Even the top athletes, business builders, Hollywood stars and financiers are not born with a positive attitude. Rather, each of them learn certain skills and develop certain habits that lead to them appearing to be extremely "lucky". They aren't lucky; they just have the right habits. That's good news because everyone can develop the habit of positive thinking.

Habits are formed by association. Negative thinking is a habit because most individuals make the association between what they are thinking and their current situation, which usually isn't as good as we'd hope for. Let me share an example.

REAL WORLD

Jerry* was an acquaintance that attended several of the same networking groups I did. He was always extremely positive and upbeat. It seemed as if nothing could go wrong for this guy. He regularly challenged others he met to shift their thinking so that it was more positive. He definitely radiated positive thoughts! By all accounts, everyone considered Jerry to be successful.

But then I stopped seeing Jerry at the events. He wasn't around anymore. One day, I wondered what he was up to and had a need to contact him so I gave him a call. Jerry didn't give me the warmest reception. His attitude was anything but positive. He was the complete opposite of the person I had come to know as he was full of complaints and blame for his bad situation. Why had someone who had been incredibly positive and upbeat become so negative?

Jerry was attempting to do what all the gurus, motivational speakers and coaches told him to do. He was thinking positively. Or at least he was attempting to control his negative thoughts. Controlling our thoughts is like building a temporary dam and using it to hold back a river of water: It will work for a short period of time but eventually the prevailing negative thoughts will break through, pulling us right back down to where we started.

Thought control is temporary. Forcing yourself to cancel negative thoughts and replace them with positive thoughts will not last long unless you can understand what caused the negative thoughts in the first place and then acknowledge that the thoughts are not relevant to you or the way you want to live your life. When we think positive thoughts and have positive results, an association is formed that reinforces the habit of positive thinking. Jerry didn't associate his positive thoughts with positive results. Without validation for those thoughts, and with the continued validation of the negative thoughts, the habit of negative thinking was stronger than the habit of positive thinking.

With the right skills, you can choose to create a habit of positive thinking.

ACTION STEP

As you begin to incorporate your new positive thoughts, look for the results. Find examples of how those thoughts served you. Write these down in a journal or notebook. By first seeking out, then finding and finally recording the results, it will create a subconscious connection between what you are doing and what you hope it will create for you.

"Any act often repeated soon forms a habit; and habit allowed, steadily gains in strength. At first it may be but as the spider's web, easily broken through, but if not resisted it soon binds us with chains of steel."

\- Tryon Edwards

Remember, it takes practice.

4

POSITIVE THINKING IS A CHOICE

"It is our choices that show what we truly are,
far more than our abilities."
- Joanne Kathleen Rowling

Choice. We all have it. We may not like it but it is ours.
There is a classic song by Rush called *Freewill* that says, "If you
choose not to decide, you still have made a choice." Not
choosing to work through your thoughts and keep them
positive is a choice to allow those thoughts to take their own,
natural course. A course that is likely not serving you well or
you wouldn't be reading this book.

Life is full of choices and choosing to be positive is just one of them. That's actually really good news. It means you don't HAVE to be negative. Stinking thinking isn't something you are stuck with.

STORY TIME

There once was a farmer who owned a donkey. One day the donkey fell into the farmer's old well. The farmer tried and tried to figure out how to rescue the donkey from the well but eventually determined that neither the well nor the donkey were worth the time or expense to save.

The farmer decided he would bury the donkey in the well to put the donkey out of its misery. He began to shovel dirt into the well. Initially, the donkey went into panic afraid of his impending death. The donkey began to shiver and shake. Then the donkey realized that, with each shake of his body, the dirt fell down to the ground raising the ground up just a little bit higher. It was then he decided he would just Shake it off and Step Up with each shovel of dirt.

With each shovel meant to put him to his death, the donkey fought the panic and took the fearful step up. Over and over again, the donkey would feel each shovel of dirt and Shake it off and step up, until, at last, the donkey reached the top of the well and stepped over the edge.

Every shovel of dirt that was meant to bury the donkey served to help him live. If the donkey had continued to stay negative, he would have not seen his opportunity to turn the negative into a positive that would save his life.

The challenge, however, is making that choice. When we feel like we are at or near our lowest point; making the choice to look at things differently, more positively, can be overwhelming. I can remember back to some of my darkest days when I would think to myself about all the "right" things to do to pull myself out of it and also thinking to myself that I didn't care. At that point I wanted to be depressed. Now I know a little secret. That need to be depressed is temporary and, on a temporary basis, it's okay. Now, rather than beating myself up about feeling that way, I give myself a certain amount of time. Sometimes it's an hour, sometimes it may be a couple of days. Once that time has passed, I start going through my choices again and realize it is now much easier to make the choice to be positive.

It is okay to have times when you are angry or sad or negative. You don't have to be positive 100% of the time. Remember, no one is. By allowing yourself to feel the entire range of feelings, you will actually choose to experience positive thoughts more frequently.

ACTION STEP

Review your options. Look carefully as, initially, it may seem as though there are none. If you don't see the choices available to you, find someone that can help point them out. Carefully consider all possible choices before making your decision. Know that at any given point, you can make a new decision based on your new circumstances.

Remember, it takes practice.

5

POSITIVE THINKING IS A JOURNEY, ENJOY THE RIDE

"The road of life twists and turns and no two directions are ever the same. Yet our lessons come from the journey, not the destination."

-Don Williams, Jr.

Because it requires making a conscious choice and takes time to create a habit, positive thinking is more like a journey than a destination. We never arrive at the Land of Positive Thinking; rather, we travel the roads named Positive Thoughts with many detours onto side streets along the way. These detours might be called Lost Job Lane, Divorce Drive or Broken Dreams Boulevard. It's tempting to allow these detours to take us in a different direction than we wanted to go much like that side road of the old days.

Think back to your childhood journeys, the family vacations in the station wagon. If you are too young to remember, go watch an old movie called National Lampoon's Vacation. You'll get the idea.

More often than not on those vacations, our parents shared with us the exciting details of where we were going but nothing about the stops along the way. We would pile into the station wagon with our games and toys to keep boredom at bay and ask every 20 minutes, "Are we there yet?" while driving our parents and siblings crazy.

When Dad decided to take a side road to visit the World's Largest Ball of String (which is located in Brooks, Missouri in case you were wondering), it was an annoying detour that delayed us from reaching the excitement promised to us upon our arrival at our final destination whether that destination was Disneyland or the Grand Canyon.

Those family vacations set a bad precedent for all of our future journeys. Anything that was not on the quickest path to the destination was bound to bring boredom and frustration. It's no wonder we look at detours off the main road with such negativity today.

What if, instead, our parents had told us about all the exciting places we would be stopping along the way and all the new adventures we would have in the process? What if we learned to look at those detours as an opportunity to learn something new or see something exciting? What if the journey was the adventure and the destination was just the end of one adventure and the beginning of another? How different would our family vacations be then? And how much better would all of our personal life journeys be now? Think about that for just a little while.

ACTION STEP

Look at positive thinking as your own little journey and each detour into negative thinking is an opportunity to see how far you still get to go. The detours are a chance to learn and grow. After all, if we aren't growing, we're dying.

Create a road map of your life. Draw the starting point, otherwise known as your birthday, and the finish line or where you'd like to end your days. Between the two points, draw all of the roads on which you have had to take a detour . These detours might include major moves, having children, not finishing college, getting turned down for a big sale or job promotion or even the death of a loved one. Fill in all of the special places you got to visit along your journey of life. Where did those detours take you and what little hidden treasure did you find there?

Begin to look at this road map as a treasure map. Each little stop has the treasure you seek even if you didn't know you should be looking. Have fun and enjoy the journey.

Remember, it takes practice.

6

POSITIVE THINKING IS ABOUT PERSPECTIVE

"Nothing in life has any real meaning except the meaning you give it." -
Tony Robbins

Try this little experiment at home. Hold up a coin by the
edge between two fingers so that you can only see the side with
"heads." Have someone stand on the other side so that they
can only see the side with "tails." Now convince the other
person that the coin is heads. To you, it certainly is. To the
other person, it is not. It all depends on what side of the coin
you are standing. It all depends on your perspective.

No matter what event occurs in your life, there are multiple ways to look at it. To one individual, a job loss is the end of the world. They have lost their livelihood, their ability to provide for their family, their purpose. To another individual, however, a job loss means new opportunities and possibilities. They have been given a chance to pursue a new direction or discover a new career. They hated the job and just didn't know how to take the step necessary to move on. These are two people with very different responses to the same situation.

REAL WORLD

Linda* was sharing with me how she just didn't understand why her sister repeatedly made what Linda assumed was a bad choice. No matter how many times Linda tried to tell her sister that she shouldn't do something the way she was, Linda's sister would persist in doing it the same way believing her way to be right.

What Linda didn't realize is that she was looking at the situation from her own perspective based on her own life experiences. I had Linda talk about how her life had been different from her sisters and begin to help her see how this might affect her sister's choices. Basically, I had Linda walk a mile in her sister's shoes. Once Linda could understand why her sister was making the choice she was, Linda was able to determine that she still did not think her sister was making a good choice. I then encouraged Linda to help her sister work through the same process and guiding her sister to understand why Linda thought it wasn't a good choice.

By first understanding from her sister's perspective, Linda was able to determine if the issue was really worth the stress she was experiencing. She was then able to help her sister have a different perspective, Linda was able to help her sister understand where Linda was coming from.

While the sisters continued to hold their old beliefs, they came to terms with their disagreement and at least understood why they saw things differently. They no longer argue about it and have a new sense of acceptance for the other's choices. This exercise allowed them to have a more positive perspective on the situation.

Have you ever had one of those days where you thought you must have woken up on the wrong side of the bed because nothing seemed to be going right that day? First, you trip over the pile of clothes left on the floor from the night before, then you get in the shower to find the shampoo bottle empty. You make it downstairs to find that the coffee pot didn't get turned on and you are already running late for work. The rest of the day doesn't seem to go much better. What if many of those things are things that you regularly experience and just tend not to focus on? When you put all the bad experiences together you notice them more and you begin to look for even more bad things that are going to happen to you that day.

There is a lot of talk about how we attract things in our lives. If we focus on good things, we get more good things and if we focus on the bad, well, we get more bad. It doesn't have anything to do with attraction. We aren't magnets in that sense with one side being the positive attracting energy and the other being the negative attracting energy. In fact, every situation is equal until we give it meaning.

The Candy Store

We are like little children in a candy store. We consume rather than attract and we tend to have a preferred candy that we go after. Our candy is either a positive perspective or a negative perspective. We thrive on that flavor and seek out more of it. Just like the children in the candy store, if we get hungry, we will go get more of our favorite candy.

Positive candy allows us to see the good things in every situation. The job loss is an opportunity to explore new paths. The rush hour traffic saves us from a car accident or speeding ticket. The extra unforeseen expense that comes up reminds us to be grateful for all we have. We eat up these positive reflections and seek out more and more of them. Those of us with this kind of positive attitude towards experiences are considered optimists, or just darn lucky.

Negative candy causes us to always find the worst in situations. The tough breaks, the bad luck. This is where we wonder why everything happens to us and why is life so unfair. Even the positive things that happen are usually "too good to be true". The person that chooses the negative perspective has a lot of negative things to say about those with more of anything than they have. This is the pessimist and they usually try to bring everyone else down to their level.

We may occasionally reach into a different candy bin but we naturally gravitate towards our preferred flavor.

Tastes Change

Every time I ask my 15 year old if he wants something to eat it seems he says he wants something he never liked before. When I tell him he didn't like that his response to me is always, "Tastes change, Mom."

That's good news for those that prefer the negative flavor. Eventually, they may decide they prefer to try something new

ACTION STEP

For the next 24 hours, challenge yourself to pay attention to every situation for which you have a negative response. Be open to the possibilities that situation may allow for. Consider all the alternatives that it could mean. Get creative. The alternatives don't have to be accurate, just another possibility. This exercise takes practice. The longer you do it, the easier it gets. Stop yourself whenever you begin to think negatively and challenge those thoughts.

Is that really the meaning you want to give to that situation? What other meanings might it have?

If you were someone else, what meaning might they give it?

At this early stage, you don't have to believe the meanings you WANT to give those negative experiences, just begin to look for and find those meanings. Eventually, your tastes will begin to change and you will start to believe the new meanings.

Remember, it takes practice.

7

POSITIVE THINKING IS RELATIVE

"Nothing has meaning except the meaning we give it."
– T. Harv Eker

Think about this: Do you believe your house is big or small?

Now what if you compared it to something else? What if you compare it to a mansion in Beverly Hills? Or how about a hut in South Africa?

Your house hasn't changed in size. It is still the same as when you first answered the question with your gut response. The only thing that has changed is how you view your house.

Initially, you had an idea of how big your house was based on experiences in your life.

I think I live in a pretty big house. It's 4500 square feet. I base my opinion on those individuals in my life whose homes I have visited. Only a couple of my friends and relatives live in bigger homes than I do. Therefore, I consider this a large home. It is fully based on my experiences of homes of people I know.

However, when I compare it to a mansion in Beverly Hills that may be more than 10,000 square feet, my home is small. The size of my home is relative to what I am comparing it to. It is neither big nor small until I give it that definition.

Just as you base your opinion of the size of your home on your experiences and attach a meaning to it, so do you base your thoughts. An event that happens in your life is neither positive nor negative until you attach a meaning to it. We tend to attach meanings based on our experiences but we always have a choice in what we compare our situations to.

Let's go back to our house example. When you look at your house now, do you decide to compare it to the mansion in Beverly Hills or the hut in South Africa? Which comparison makes you feel good and positive? Is that the one you are choosing or are you choosing to compare your home to the one that makes you feel bad and negative?

In 1946, Victor Frankl published a book entitled, *Man's Search for Meaning*. Frankl had been a Jewish Psychiatrist and a Holocaust survivor. In his book, Frankl describes his life in a concentration camp and his theory on finding the meaning in everything, even the most horrible experiences of life. The prisoners of these camps did not have a choice to be there. The actual situation that they were in was beyond their control. Frankl's book shows us that we can't avoid the horrible experiences and the pain they may cause but we can choose the meaning we give those circumstances.

We can even choose not to attach any meaning at all.

STORY TIME

This is the story from Zen and Taoism of an old farmer who had worked his crops for many years. One day his horse ran away. Upon hearing the news, his neighbors came to visit.

"Such bad luck," they said sympathetically.

"We'll see," the farmer replied.

The next morning the horse returned, bringing with it three other wild horses.

"How wonderful," the neighbors exclaimed.

"We'll see," replied the old man.

The following day, his son tried to ride one of the untamed horses, was thrown, and broke his leg. The neighbors again came to offer their sympathy on his misfortune.

"We'll see," answered the farmer.

The day after, military officials came to the village to draft young men into the army. Seeing that the son's leg was broken, they passed him by. The neighbors congratulated the farmer on how well things had turned out.

"We'll see," said the farmer.

This farmer did not give meaning to any of the incidents in his life. He could have allowed the meaning of his neighbors to be his own but chose, instead to allow the events to play out without determining them to be either good or bad.

While the farmer gave no meaning to the events, you can choose to only give a positive meaning to the events in your life. Everything that happens to us can be positive when compared to the right situation. It's up to you to decide to what you will compare your experiences.

ACTION STEP

Norman Vincent Peale said, "Become a possibilitarian. No matter how dark things seem to be or actually are, raise your sights and see possibilities - always see them, for they're always there." I couldn't think of better advice than this!

Choose to give your thoughts a positive spin instead of a negative one. Here are some examples.

The negative thought (NT) – If I quit or get fired, I'll never find another job.

The positive spin (PS)– Being out of this job gives me the opportunity to move into an area that I've always been interested in.

NT – I don't have enough money.

PS – I choose to spend my money in other ways at this time.

NT – No one is buying homes right now.

PS – The unqualified buyers have quit looking, freeing my time for only the most qualified clients.

NT – I can't afford to go to college.

PS – Poorer people than myself have made it through four years plus of a college education. If they can do it, so can I!

NT – My life couldn't get any worse.

PS – I'm grateful that I have this opportunity to grow and know the positive change will come very soon.

NT – I have to wait to do that.

PS – There is no better time than now.

NT – No one likes me.

PS – I can't please everyone so I'll only focus on the important ones.

NT – I just can't stop this negative thinking!

PS – I know it won't happen overnight, so I will celebrate each negative thought that I am able to turn around today.

Now practice writing some of your own with your most dominant negative thoughts. Writing these in advance will help you to quickly think of them when the thoughts pop up.

Remember, it takes practice.

8

SHIFT YOUR ATTITUDE WITH GRATITUDE

"When you are grateful, fear disappears and abundance appears."
- Anthony Robbins

A positive attitude is far easier to obtain when we are grateful for the things we currently have in our lives. I feel this is such an important step that I make it the first lesson I teach to my new coaching clients. I guide them through the process of finding at least one thing to be grateful for every single day.

Sometimes finding gratitude has to start very small. It can be something as small as having food to eat today or clothes to wear. It isn't important how insignificant you may feel the gratitude is because, when you really look at it, you can see that there are other humans somewhere in this world that do not even have the most basic needs met. Somewhere, there is someone that does not have a meal to eat today or shoes for their feet. Somewhere there is someone that can't walk or even get out of bed. Somewhere there is someone that is terminally ill. Therefore, having food to eat or shoes and clothes is something for which to be grateful. Having the ability to need shoes to walk and the health to continue walking into the future are truly wonderful things for which to be grateful.

Here's a quick list of things you can focus your gratitude towards:

- Health - It may not be perfect but at least you aren't dead.
- Food to eat
- Air to breath
- A roof over your head
- A smile
- A shower
- A smile from a loved one
- A bed to sleep in
- The sun shining
- A good movie or a great book

There are some individuals, however, that are so bogged down in their misery that they struggle to even see the very basic gifts they have as being worthy of their gratitude. Rather than seeing the benefit of the food they have to eat, they see the struggle it was to obtain the food. Rather than feeling the comfort of the shoes on their feet, they complain that a new pair costs too much. Rather than being grateful for the ability to walk and live, they find these things to be a burden. They feel that if they have so many struggles, then the little things just don't matter.

This ungratefulness is truly a victim's mentality. A victim dismisses the little things because they believe it won't affect the outcome anyway. Their expectations are high that they be given exactly what they deserve. What they are missing is that they are given exactly what they deserve.

If you find yourself dismissing these things as insignificant and unworthy of your gratitude, you may find yourself struggling to succeed at anything in life. This is not the time for "Ya, buts…". Rather, it is a time to let go of all your worry, blame and doubt and feel the gifts you have been given.

Life is full of challenges, struggles, times of extreme stress and turmoil. Those that succeed are those that can be grateful despite these challenging times. The ones that take ownership of their own destiny and realize that the first step to reversing their current status is to be grateful for all of the things they still have, no matter how insignificant it may feel.

The Law of Attraction

Now, before you make assumptions and skip this section, read it with an open mind. You may learn something you never thought of before.

There is a phenomenon called the Law of Attraction that occurs when someone thinks a certain way. They then tend to continue to see things based on that thought process and are unable to change the course of events. If those thoughts are that nothing is good or worthy of gratitude, then they will miss the fortunes they already have in their life and all the new fortunes that come their way.

However, if the thoughts are about what is still good and all of the fortunes they still have, they begin to see new opportunities and new experiences as new gifts and more positive experiences come their way. It's like when you get a brand new car. Before buying that car, you hadn't seen anything quite like it, but after… All of a sudden this car seems to be EVERYWHERE. The Law of Attraction really works because our focus is shifted to look for different things.

Through shifting your focus on being grateful for what you already have, it is far easier to shift your attitude into a positive state. How can you feel negative when you have even just one thing that draws your gratitude and that's what you choose for your focus? Your new gratitude can carry throughout the day shifting your attitude at any point that you most need it.

REAL WORLD

In the month of November a couple of years ago, I noticed someone on Facebook posting something they were grateful for each day of that month in honor of Thanksgiving. I really liked that idea and decided to try it out for myself. At the end of the month, I felt better and thought it was such a good idea, I'd continue it till the end of the year. I've never stopped. Almost every single day, I log on to Facebook and post one thing I'm grateful for that day. It has become my own personal gratitude journal.

Several of my friends online have said that my gratitudes inspire them. That's wonderful to know, but what truly keeps me doing it is how they make me feel. Each day, when I sit down to post my gratitude, I have easily a dozen or more ideas pop into my head. Which one gets top billing today? I love the feeling of appreciation and the ongoing mood it puts me in when I post them. There is also a side benefit of using Facebook for my gratitude journal: whenever someone else reads my posting and comments on it, I get uplifted all over again!

When I am feeling very stressed and the Facebook posts just aren't cutting it, I will often sit down and write at least 100 gratitudes. I make sure not to duplicate or even have things very similar. For example, I don't allow myself to be grateful for ice cream and cake but dessert in general. This process can be time consuming and difficult but it always makes me think of the wonderful things I have in my life and allows me to reflect on what is truly important.

When we are fully present and thinking about the wonderful things we have in our life, it is impossible to think about the negative things. One mind cannot have two thoughts at the exact same moment. The more we shift our focus to gratitude, the less we will dwell on negative experiences and the more positive we will become.

ACTION STEP

Journaling isn't for everyone and you have probably already figured out how to do that on your own so I won't bore you with that whole exercise again. First, though, I do want to give you a few outside-the-box ways to journal. Then I will give you another exercise if journaling just isn't for you.

Alternative Ways to Journal

Video journal – record your gratitudes to a video recorder and post them on Facebook, Youtube or just keep them for yourself. Many phones these days have video recorders or you can purchase one fairly inexpensively.

Facebook or Twitter posts – You are welcome to adopt my own journaling style and use social media.

Text your gratitude – Have someone close to you be your recipient and text your gratitude each day to that person.

Other Ideas

Marbles, stones or chips – Each day, take a marble, small stone, poker chip or even a penny and state your gratitude while holding the item. Then place the item in a clear glass jar or vase. You may also choose to place the stones in a small garden where you can go to be at peace. Watch the gratitudes accumulate. Using pennies also helps grow that financial savings account!

The Gratitude Police – This idea works great if you have children or a helpful spouse. Share your idea with your police force. Have them encourage you to be grateful each day. For every negative thing you say, have them encourage you to state two gratitudes. You won't be complaining for long!

Remember, it takes practice!

9

TAKING ADVANTAGE OF THE BUTTERFLY EFFECT

"Shallow men believe in luck, believe in circumstances.
Strong men believe in cause and effect."

-Ralph Waldo Emerson

There is a theory that if a butterfly flaps its wings in Brazil, it could cause a tornado in Texas. The Theory of Sensitive Dependence on Initial Conditions (I know, that's a mouth full) indicates that the slightest change from the initial set of conditions can produce vast long-term changes in the end result. This is more frequently called the Butterfly Effect and refers to the idea that seemingly insignificant events can cause very significant outcomes.

TRUE STORY

There are interesting stories that trace the lineage of the Butterfly Effect back at least three generations. These stories show how one little choice has potentially altered the entire history of the world. Take, for example, the story of Colonel Joshua Chamberlain.

Before the Civil War, Colonel Chamberlain was a college professor with no prior military training. Despite this fact, he performed his duties as a military officer with a high level of dedication. During the Battle of Gettysburg, Colonel Chamberlain was faced with a certain defeat. He and his troops were outnumbered and the ammunition supplies were running low. After several advances, the South had inflicted a great deal of damage causing the North to lose hundreds of men. In the face of terrible odds and almost certain death, Colonel Chamberlain pushed forth. During one assault, Colonel Chamberlain was shot at being struck on his heavy metal belt buckle. If the shot had struck a fraction of an inch in a different direction, Colonel Chamberlain would have been wounded and taken out of the battle.

Colonel Chamberlain understood the significance of Gettysburg and knew that the hill must be won. With ammunition running low and troops being few, Colonel Chamberlain ordered a charge "at bayonet," meaning they would fight with the knives on their guns. This one order was enough to secure the victory at Gettysburg.

It is interesting to note that many historians believe that if Gettysburg had not been won, the Confederate would have won the war. The historians also speculate that if the South had won the war, we would not be split into two separate countries but rather split into several countries more like Europe. Should this have occurred, it is unlikely that any one of these smaller countries would have been the super power able to defeat Hitler and Japan during World War II. Democracy as we know it today would certainly not exist.

All of this because of the decision of one man to not give up and retreat but rather to move forward in spite of terrible odds.

Life is made up of a series of choices. Each day we make hundreds of choices; which route do we drive, what do we eat, what radio station do we listen to, what activities we do and which ones we put off, whether or not we smile, how we treat others, etc... The choices we make, no matter how insignificant they may seem, mold and shape us.

It may seem that smiling or not smiling to the person that makes our Caramel Macchiato in the morning would not be a life changing event. In fact, that one little thing, taken as an isolated incident entirely lacking all other experiences in our lives, would not be life changing. However, what if that one smile determined your mood for the day and your mood allowed you to close a big sale or connect with someone meant to be your future spouse? What if that one smile lead to something amazing.

While you may never agree that the flap of a butterfly's wings in Brazil could create a tornado in Texas, I'd like to argue that one little smile, a left turn here instead of there, rush hour traffic; it all has a cause and effect. Most people would not disagree that we have days where it just seems we got up on the wrong side of the bed. Isn't it possible that one simple act in the earliest part of our day, triggered a chain reaction of events that caused us to wish we could just go back to bed? Then it can certainly also act the opposite way.

If you accept that a small early morning event could cause a series of "bad day" experiences, then allow yourself to believe that it is also possible that CHOOSING to have one small positive experience could turn your whole day around.

ACTION STEP

The next time things don't seem to be going your way, make a conscious decision to create a positive experience. There are many things you can do that will create a positive energy within you. Try one of these or think of your own:

- Smile at someone
- Say Hi to someone
- Pay someone a compliment
- Send someone a thank you note
- Take a moment to do something you love
- List 10 things you are grateful for
- Help someone do something
- Hug a loved one
- Make a call you know will be good
- Complete one major to-do item on your list
- Sing a song
- Dance
- Choose to do something completely the opposite of what you would normally do.

Choosing to do one or more of these things may be very hard to do at first, but do it. Once you have made the choice and taken the action, pay attention to how you feel and what good things are happening around you.

If the action does not result in positive feelings, try something else on the list. If the feeling is positive then continue through your day and see just how much positive energy is attracted to you.

This process allows you to take advantage of the Butterfly Effect. It allows you to make a deliberate choice that results in a chain reaction of positive events throughout the rest of your day. Now THAT'S power!

Remember, it takes practice.

10

THE LAW OF DUALITY

Duality is the notion that you cannot have one without the
opposite also being present. Left, right; up, down; day, night.
You can't have one without the other. These are simple
examples. Some of the more profound include right, wrong;
good, bad; love, hate. When you begin to understand that you
cannot have love without hate, right without wrong or good
without bad; it begins to help you accept those opposite results,
embrace them for what they are and what they will soon bring
and move past them.

We often beat ourselves up when we have bad days. It is
easy to become frustrated when nothing seems to be going

your way. We start to talk about just wanting to call in sick and go back to bed. However, when you begin to think about how that bad day must be present in some form to have the good days, it becomes a little easier to deal with. This new insight is often just what it takes to reverse the bad tide and make the day just a little brighter.

REAL WORLD

Cindy* was working on a very large project. When she finally completed the project, Cindy shared it with her husband. Immediately, she felt let down as she didn't get the response she expected from her husband. Cindy really wanted someone, specifically him, to give her a big hug and tell her how awesome she was. Instead she got a quick, "that's great, hon" before he moved on with what he was doing.

After several similar reactions and much contemplation on her part, she shared her concerns with me. Together, we were able to look at this negative situation for what it was and help her find the necessary support elsewhere.

The next week, Cindy reported to me that her husband had made a complete turnaround. He was now more supportive than ever and made extra efforts to encourage her and help her celebrate her success.

Cindy's pendulum swung both ways. By taking a breath and knowing that it would soon shift, she was able to maintain her positivity despite what she felt as a lack of support.

Duality also affects our choices. When negative things begin to happen in our lives, the human spirit tends to pull back towards the center. We do not want to be on the negative side of duality for long therefore we make strides to swing things into the positive side of the pendulum and keep it there as long as we can. Therefore our choices reflect that draw towards the positive side and sometimes even towards the center. Consider the friend of yours that no matter how many times they fall in love, they tend to sabotage the results? This friend is drawing back towards the center and not allowing themselves to continue to experience the side of the pendulum that is most in their benefit.

You might be wondering why this is a good thing. How can the idea that you have to be on both sides of the pendulum be positive for you?

Look deeper. Utilizing the Law of Duality does not mean that, in order to be really rich, you must also be really poor at some point as well. Rather, it means that some experience may occur within your life that could be interpreted as you being poor. Do you remember when we talked about positive thinking being relative? Nothing has meaning except the meaning we give it. When we can just accept that this law is a part of our life, it helps us to take a more positive perspective on every situation. Perhaps the key to using this principle in your favor is to understand that it exists, using that knowledge to reduce or eliminate some of the anxiety associated with the negative sides of the pendulum and then to begin using it in your favor to swing the pendulum in your preferred direction by seeking out paths to the other side.

11

EVERYTHING HAPPENS FOR A REASON

"Everything happens for a reason and a purpose, and it serves you."
- Anthony Robbins

Everything happens for a reason. Every action has a reaction. Always remember that what's meant to be will always find a way to come about and that's the really good news.

I recently learned to really absorb and latch on to this idea while driving down the road in rush hour traffic. My husband and I had just dropped off my 14 year old son for a school dance. I walked him into the dance. Once inside, he realized he had left his wallet in the car. I had to run back to the car to retrieve his wallet for him. I don't remember why but we were in a bit of a hurry, so this delay was just a bit frustrating.

I got back in the car to hurry to our destination. Not five minutes after getting on the freeway, traffic came to an abrupt halt. It wasn't a slow trickle, it was a dead stop. It took us about 15 minutes to travel one mile before we reached the reason for the delay; a major, multi-vehicle fatal car crash that was about to shut down the freeway completely for several hours.

One mile was all that separated us from being involved in that fatal accident. One mile. Five minutes. If my son had not left his wallet in the car and we had left just 5 minutes earlier, we would have been right in the thick of that accident and I might have a much more unpleasant story to tell.

The trivial details of our lives are what create the ultimate outcomes. That butterfly effect of one forgotten wallet shaped the future events of my life and the lives of those around me. Everything in this world happens for a reason. We don't always know the reason or have a clear understanding of it. The good news is that we don't have to. It just is.

While everything does happen for a reason, that does not mean we have no control over our destinies. Rather, our actions dictate how things will play out. If we take action in our lives to create positive change, then life rewards us with experiences that will be positive for us either through a lesson, a positive experience or a saving grace. It's all in how you choose to look at it?

REAL WORLD

Jack* was a coaching client that would regularly get frustrated by missed appointments and no shows. He began calculating the percentage of people that didn't call or show up to meetings he had scheduled. He would come to me at each coaching session to share what the previous week's percentage was, like a badge of some sort. "This week it was 27% no show."

While I can certainly understand the frustration one feels when their time is taken up to drive to a location and sit waiting, dwelling on the negative isn't the best use of our time either. I asked Jack if there had ever been a time where someone did not initially show up to a meeting and, when they finally did connect, the results were spectacular! Or possibly a time when there was a no show but Jack ended up connecting with someone else in that amount of time leading to something wonderful.

Jack could actually remember a few such occasions including one where he was able to sign a big deal with a contact who initially had to cancel due to a death in the family. Because of this, Jack began to realize that it is often the best possible scenario when someone doesn't show up at a specific time or place. He began to actually look at no shows entirely differently, like it was perfectly okay because it was allowing a better experience to come along.

Jack then began calling his missed appointments to thank them for a valuable opportunity, either one in which he was able to do something in that time that he normally wouldn't have or that they would have a much more productive meeting when they did finally meet.

Can you guess what happened? Yep, Jack's no show percentage dropped to just over 3% and the ones that didn't make it called to let Jack know why well in advance.

We don't always know WHY things happen the way they do. We won't always be able to determine where the hidden benefit lies. Sometimes, it is enough to know it is there keeping us on the right path no matter what obstacles are thrown in our way. Sometimes we have to be a little creative in making "stuff" up that our logical brains can feel comfortable with even if it isn't the truth. The great thing is, whatever we make up, doesn't have to be accurate, it just has to sound good. Have you ever wanted to live the life of a movie writer or novelist? Now's your chance.

ACTION STEP

Practice finding a positive spin for all the little situations you come across. I started with reminding myself why traffic was a good thing for me and the reasons included:

1. No speeding tickets
2. Less risk of accidents, especially serious ones
3. More time to listen to my taped seminars and books
4. Getting the timing right to meet the right person when I'm supposed to.

Another example might be why you didn't get the raise you were hoping for. Some possible examples of why this might be a good thing include:

1. You seek out additional training that lands you a better job rather than just a raise
2. You choose to go out and look for a better opportunity
3. You were about to be audited by the IRS and this would have put you on the fast track list
4. Because you didn't get your raise, your spouse asks for one at their position which results in a bigger income overall.

These are just a few quick ones. There are always a large number of reasons we could come up with if we give it enough time and enough creativity.

Practicing this skill will help you to do it automatically and help the creativity get easier. So go out there and get wild and crazy and start making stuff up! What do you have to lose? We don't always need a reason for something, but it often helps.

Remember, it takes practice.

12

RECHARGING YOUR BATTERIES

"Should the cabin lose pressure, oxygen masks will drop from the overhead area. Please place the bag over your own mouth and nose before assisting children".

One very important step in staying positive is to have time set aside to recharge our own batteries. Just like the famous safety line from every airplane flight I've ever taken suggests, take care of yourself first. You are no good to anyone dead.

Before I get too far into that though, I want to remind you; we all have the same amount of time, it just depends on what you make time for. It doesn't matter how little time you feel you have, if you learned that a loved one was critically ill in the hospital, you'd make time to go see them.

Each one of us is like a little rechargeable battery. You come from the store with a full amount of juice and ready to perform at your best. However, as you get used for various purposes (work, chores, family, friends, church, community), your energy reserves begin to drop faster and faster. You might be able to give them a bit of a recharge periodically (a nice hot bath, or some time to work on a hobby) to keep up a minimal level of energy but ultimately, it will need a full charge.

Unfortunately though, most of us don't even take time to do the brief recharge. We don't take enough time for ourselves. This is detrimental on many levels. First, lacking a recharge makes you less productive. Have you ever tried to use rechargeable batteries without a full charge in electronic equipment such as cameras? It just doesn't work! Without a full charge, you don't get as much done in as little time as you otherwise are capable of. You can't perform at your optimum levels. You can't be your best. Think of how productive you feel on your very best days? Now what if you could feel that way EVERY day? That's what a recharge on a regular basis will do for you.

When you are fully recharged, your mind is easier to direct. When you are running on reserves, it requires too much energy and mental strength to keep your mind focused on the positive.

The tiny little roots of negative energy begin to slip through the cracks of our positive attitude and begin to grow. Left unchecked, the roots will push away at the positive attitude leaving gaps to be filled by negative thoughts.

Just as Jeff Olson says, "It's easy to do. And it's easy not to do." Recharging your batteries is simple and easy to do but most people don't MAKE the time to do it. Realize that if you take one hour once a week to recharge your batteries, you will gain at least two hours of productivity each week. Therefore, you will actually have gained a full 60 minutes of time!

ACTION STEP

Each week set aside 1 to 4 hours of time for things that relax and rejuvenate you. This is time JUST for you, not family, not friends, not work or community; unless those things leave you feeling relaxed and reenergized. If, after spending time with family, you still wonder where's the "me" time, then it doesn't qualify.

Here are a few ideas of what you could do to recharge your batteries.

• Read a book
• Take a bath

- Get back to a favorite hobby
- Find a new hobby
- Get a massage
- Watch a movie
- Go for a hike
- Explore your city or town
- Listen to music

Find one thing that you truly love to do and make time for it each and every week. Your attitude will improve and your energy will go up drastically!

Remember, it takes practice.

13

RANDOM ACTS OF KINDNESS

"He who distributes the milk of human kindness
cannot help but spill a little on himself"
- James Matthew Barrie

One of the quickest and best ways to stop thinking about our own misery is to focus on how we can improve the life of someone else, even if only just for a moment. Doing good deeds or Random Acts of Kindness (RAKs) take our focus off of our own trials and tribulations, help us to see that others may be even less fortunate than ourselves and facilitate our gratitude for what is currently good in our own lives right now.

In addition, there is some scientific evidence that proves doing good for others is good for us. There was a study conducted at the Washington University School of Medicine in St. Louis, Missouri[1] which showed that when brains are scanned with Magnetic Resonance Imaging (MRI) while making charitable donations vs refusing to make charitable donations, the same area of the brain which is affected by receiving monetary rewards also lights up with the giving of charitable donations. Giving and helping others makes us feel just as good as receiving financial rewards.

Good acts can come in many forms such as monetary donations, time or prayers. Each form has benefits and no form is necessarily better than the other.

Performing good acts is a win-win.

ACTION STEP

This one is simple. Make it a point to perform various acts of kindness. These can be long-term commitments to non-profit agencies or quick, two-second acts that have long term effects. Here are some suggestions for the small RAKs:

- Buy a dozen flowers and hand them out at random.

- Pay for someone's toll behind you.

- Help someone across the street.

- Gather a few neighbors to help clean up the worst yard on the block.

- Leave an anonymous note for a co-worker telling them what you value in them.

- Ask the grocery store clerk how their day is before they ask you and ask with sincerity.

In addition, there are a great number of charity organizations that could use your donation of time and/or money. Consider some of these great charities:

- Dreamchaser PMU Horse Rescue, www.dreamchaserpmu.org or another animal rescue organization near you.

- Singleton Moms, www.singletonmoms.org Supporting single parents with cancer.

- Junior Achievement, www.ja.org. Educating children in financial literacy.

- Or use a service like Volunteer Match, www.volunteermatch.org, to find a need in your area.

Taking a few moments or even a few hours a week to think about someone else's needs may be the greatest boost to your own positive outlook you'll find. It is just like taking a drug only without all the side effects.

Remember, it takes practice.

14

UNDERSTANDING VS ACCEPTING

"It is the mark of an educated mind
to be able to entertain a thought without accepting it."
— Aristotle

One of the big challenges we often face in life is how to handle other people. As a life coach, I see the struggles that people face and the negative thoughts and attitudes that result when they are confronted with someone that they don't know how to deal with. Sometimes, my client sees the other person as "in the wrong" or stubborn or just dumb sometimes. They want to know how to change the person. Fortunately, because otherwise people would be changing us all the time too, we can't change others, we can only change ourselves.

We become our best in life, not when we try to change others, but when we seek to change ourselves.

REAL WORLD

I have a client, Melissa*, whose sister Jen* is the very opposite of herself. Money, religion, education, everything. Melissa recently experienced a situation in which Jen did something that just dumbfounded Melissa and went against everything that Melissa believes. Melissa came to me wondering what she could do to make Jen see the error of her ways.

The first step I took with Melissa was to show her all of the ways their experiences differed as she and Jen grew up. I showed her how Jen was not the same as she was and all of Jen's current beliefs were a result of Jen's experiences while Melissa's beliefs were a result of Melissa's experiences. In essence, I had Melissa walk a mile in Jen's footsteps.

Once Melissa was able to see that she and Jen were two entirely different people, she had a better understanding of why she was unable to convince Jen to behave differently. They had different ideas of what was right. Neither was wrong for their own situation and neither was right for the other's situation.

Understanding is different than accepting. Understanding simply means that you realize you are different and that, if you had lived in that person's life, you may possibly make the same choices they do. Accepting means that you agree to or consent to the choices they are making. We always want to strive for understanding but we do not always need to, nor should we always, accept the choices a person makes.

Understanding simply comes from knowing that they are not you and that their experiences lend to a different set of beliefs. It is an incredibly powerful skill and those who can master it, raise to a much higher level of wisdom and growth. With this understanding, we can give up the struggle to be right thus freeing ourselves from the negative thoughts and attitudes that this struggle brings.

ACTION STEP

Consider a current person you are having a hard time dealing with. Take a moment to put your creative hat on and pretend to be that person. Think about what you know about this person and the experiences they have had in their life.

Take out a piece of paper and write down a personal history of this person as if you were the person. While pretending to be this person, explain, via a personal history, why you are the way you are. If there has been a specific situation that this person has done to cause a problem for you, write an explanation from their perspective on why they did it the way they did.

The story you write does not need to be accurate. You get to be a movie script writer and make it up as you go along. The idea is just to plant the seeds within your mind that there are potential reasons that this person has made the choices they have and that their choices are not about you.

Once you have completed the exercise, feel free to burn, bury or flush the evidence.

Remember, it takes practice.

15

STAYING POSITIVE AROUND NEGATIVE PEOPLE

"I have never met a man so ignorant
that I couldn't learn something from him."
- Galileo Galilei

It's not uncommon for my coaching clients to share with me that the ones they love the most; spouses, parents, children, dear friends, don't support their efforts for positive growth. In fact, this is also probably the most frequently asked question I receive when talking with prospective clients as well. Maintaining a positive attitude around negative people can be a struggle if the desired outcome is to have growth while also maintaining those relationships. There are times, however, when you need to look carefully at your relationships and decide if they are worth staying around. Sometimes the answer will be no. However, sometimes the answer will be yes.

Maintaining these relationships can be one of the biggest challenges you will face in your journey to being a more positive person. As your outlook on life changes, you may find that some people near to you struggle with the new you. They were comfortable with who you used to be and the new you causes them to look deeply at themselves and see things they may not like to see. It's a journey they might not be willing or ready to make themselves so their best solution is to bring you back down to their comfort zone.

It is said that you can't boil one crab at a time. If you put a single crab in a pot of boiling water, it will crawl out. However, if you place two crabs in the same pot of boiling water, they will continue to pull each other back down in their own attempts to crawl out to safety. Our closest loved ones may be much the same way. As they see us crawling out of our own misery, they will inadvertently pull us back down over and over again.

It is crucial that you recognize this and do not let this roadblock sabotage your journey. Utilize any and all of the following techniques to strengthen and persevere. The rewards will be well worth it.

ACTION STEPS

This is such an important topic that there are several steps listed here. The first one is critical. Without it, nothing else will work. Start there. Once that is in place, continue through the chain of tips. Some of them are supported by a previous tip to being completed before working on that tip.

Tip 1 - First and foremost, BE SURE of what you are doing. Have confidence in yourself and the choices you are making for your growth. If you have doubt in yourself, it makes it all that much easier for those around you to doubt the new you and the healthy choices you are making. Any little gap in your armor of confidence allows them to find your weaknesses and utilize them to pull you right back down to where you were. You MUST KNOW with all of your heart that you are doing what is best for you and those around you.

Tip 2 - Determine what lessons you can learn from your loved one. Allow their negativity to be your gift. Watch them to see what you can learn how to do differently. There are two ways we learn by example. We either learn what TO do or what NOT to do. Use this person's attitude as a lesson on what NOT to do. After all, they are displaying exactly what we are attempting to change within ourselves.

Tip 3 - Choose to believe that your loved ones truly want what is best for you and will love the new you. When you are able to believe that, then your belief will help you to see their negativity differently, more positively.

To create this belief, simply write a story that supports this belief. Make it sound like the best motion picture movie of all time. The story should be something that sounds realistic to you, that you could actually envision being true. Make it SO good that you couldn't even think about it NOT being true. Maybe their negative talk and actions that seem to encourage you to give up your positive attitude are actually their way to keep you safe from harm, just as our own fears attempt to keep us from harm. Or maybe they simply don't yet understand how the new you will be so much better for them than the old you. Once you have a story that makes logical sense, then you will have belief.

Tip 4 - Don't assume that the other person is trying to sabotage your efforts. A comment they make or an action they take may have nothing to do with you and your journey to a more positive attitude. However, you may begin to make up a story in your mind about what their comment or action means without even asking the other person for clarification. Talk to the person when they do or say something hurtful to see where they are coming from. Attempt to see things from their perspective. You may be very surprised to find out their actions either have nothing at all to do with you or that their intent was very different from what you thought.

Tip 5 - Share with the other person how you feel about their words or actions. They may not have any idea that they are being hurtful. Bringing it to their attention will help them recognize what they are doing and stop them from continuing. Help them to see things from your perspective.

One caveat; when talking to the other person, be careful to phrase your feelings in a non-threatening way. Rather than saying, "You make me feel…" Say, "When you …, I feel…, because…" For example, "when you tell me to quit wasting my time reading all these books, I feel mad that you don't understand because this is something that is important to me and I need you to support my becoming a better person." Stating your feelings in this way, allows their guard to stay down and prevents them from getting defensive. You aren't attacking them, but sharing how you feel.

You may need to gently remind them for a while as their words or actions come up. Just as it will take you practice to stay positive, so will it take them some practice as well.

Tip 6 - If the other person is truly being negative and your efforts to help them see how this affects you have not been successful, support and encourage them. There is a good chance that they have fears of their own and need some reassurance that your new positive attitude will be in their best interest as well as yours. Listen to their fears and offer guidance if they would like it. Your new found strength can be an asset for them during this challenging period. Celebrate your ability to support them in their time of need.

Tip 7 - Surround yourself with positive people in various areas of your life. Find new, more positive friends and colleagues in church groups, networking groups, hobby or activity clubs and volunteer organizations. Make contact and build relationships with people that will support and encourage you in your growth process. Find a way to spend as much time as possible with these new friends. There is some evidence that suggests you are only going to be as successful as your 5 closest friends. Who are your closest friends?

Tip 8 - Accept the negativity as a challenge. A challenge can be a great adventure and something to look forward to. If you considering the negative attitude of someone else as a challenge you must overcome for yourself, it will help you to see it in a different perspective. It becomes more of a game rather than a problem you must endure. How many ways can you think of to overcome or at least block out their negativity? Challenge yourself to think outside the box.

Tip 9 - Humor can be very valuable. Find humor in the negative attitude of others. Treat their negativity as a game. How many negative words can you count? Or add a silly phrase to the end of each of their statements. For example they might say, "Why do you spend so much money on all that self help crap?" to which you can mentally add the phrase "with whipped cream and a cherry on top."

A word of caution, however, be very careful with how you exhibit your humor. It can end up offending the other person and make the situation worse.

Tip 10 - Accept responsibility. The fact that the other person's comments or actions impact you indicates that you have an ongoing need for approval from others. It is time to believe in your own greatness and acknowledge your own worthiness. Once you can do this, you will be UNSTOPPABLE.

Bonus Tip - Hire a coach. A personal coach can help with all of the negative self talk that you do because of what you are hearing from those close to you. Sometimes your best ally is not someone that is intimate with you but removed from the daily life you lead. A coach can be extremely beneficial in helping you also know how to handle the negative person in your life.

It may take your loved ones some time to get acquainted with the new you but; time and patience will show them they have nothing to fear. Help them to embrace your new positive attitude and find ways to understand their fears. You are on this journey together.

When a close friend or relative is a negative influence on you, it does not mean you must end the relationship. Using these tools will help you to become a stronger person despite those around you. However, you may find that once you begin to blossom, you won't want to hang on to those negative influences any longer. At least then you will have the choice.

Remember, it takes practice.

16

FORGIVENESS WILL SET **YOU** FREE

Merriam-Webster defines forgive as "to give up resentment of …"

Sometimes our negative thoughts arise from the feelings of ill will we have for another person and what we *perceive* they did to us. And sometimes these thoughts come from ill will we have for ourselves. Letting go of these thoughts and feelings may make us feel like we are giving the person a free pass or excusing what they (or we) did. This just isn't so. Forgiveness is more about releasing the negative energy that is doing *us* harm.

"Holding on to anger and resentment is like drinking poison and expecting someone else to die." - Unknown

REAL WORLD

I was once asked by a coaching client, Bill* why he should forgive an old business partner that stole their business and ran it into the ground leaving Bill with nothing but a mountain of debt and a total lack of trust.

I asked Bill to make a list of how that experience was affecting him today. He listed things like still getting out of debt, not being where he planned to be, not having what he should have.

Then I gave him a few more, like not trusting, not pursuing his dreams, accepting his circumstances and allowing them to hold him back. Bob had a great deal of blame wrapped in that one experience. If it weren't for that, he believed, he could be and have all that he ever wanted.

Bill had to forgive: NOT for the benefit of the business partner whom he would never have to see or talk to again, but for his own growth.

When Bill held on to his anger and resentment he was unable to proceed with his own desires. Through some exercises, he was finally able to release those negative emotions and forgive his previous business partner and is no longer held back by that experience.

By the way, to forgive does not mean you must forget. If you choose to both forgive and forget, you may not have learned the lessons you needed to in order to avoid experiencing that situation again. History is full of forgotten lessons and repeated mistakes. Choose not to be given that painful experience all over by acknowledging and accepting the lesson.

It may be one of the hardest things you must do but true forgiveness, for those living or passed, may be a crucial step in your overall happiness and success.

ACTION STEP

Write down an inventory of who you are ready to forgive. Consider each of the individuals and think of all the positive things that may have come out of knowing that person or experiencing the situation that you feel hurt over. Find gratitude in the positive aspects of the experience knowing that they would not have been possible without the negative.

Now consider the damage that holding on to this resentment is causing you. How does it make you feel? Who is benefiting from these negative emotions? Just like you wouldn't want to give a bully the ongoing enjoyment of seeing you continue to suffer, you probably don't want the offender to have any benefit from what they have done to you.

Finally, make the choice. Is this the "gift" that will keep on "giving" or will you find happiness and joy in the true gifts you have received from the experience? The gifts of the lessons learned and the unforeseen benefits.

Remember, it takes practice.

17

BEING IN INTEGRITY

"Integrity is the essence of everything successful."
- Richard Buckminster Fuller

Integrity – adherence to moral and ethical principles;
soundness of moral character; honesty.

Being in integrity creates a positive attitude and fosters
positive thinking in two different ways. The first way is
through upholding our moral and ethical beliefs. When we are
in integrity, we do not make promises or do things that will
create ill feelings within ourselves which result in negative

thoughts and feelings. Agreeing to perform a job or function that goes against our principles is an example of being out of integrity with ourselves. Taking a job that feels good or right and rewarding allows us to stay in integrity with ourselves. Therefore, by maintaining our core values and staying in integrity, we can feel better about ourselves and attract more positive energy.

REAL WORLD

Ryan* came to me in distress over a potential client of his. This would have been a very large client for Ryan and at a time when he could really use the steady income for his business. The problem was that the prospect was working on a project to raise support for a rather controversial issue that Ryan did not agree with. In his heart, Ryan knew he should let the client know that he was not the right person for this project but his brain kept telling him that the money was more important than standing up for his beliefs.

In coaching Ryan, it came out that he had frequently taken on clients that he didn't feel good about although not to this extent. He struggled to see how avoiding those negative clients would affect other areas of his work.

With some explanation and guidance, Ryan finally decided not to work with this particular prospect. Within 24 hours of turning that one down, Ryan was approached to work with another prospect who was working on a project that was quite in sync with his own beliefs. It is likely that Ryan would not have had the time to interview the new prospect if he had accepted the first job and got to work on it. Therefore, saying no to that one, allowed him to say yes to the right one.

ACTION STEP

Know your values, moral and ethical standards and do not waver from them. There are many templates online for taking a values assessment[2]. Once you know your core values, use them as a compass to determine what choices you make in every area of your life. Celebrate each decision you make that is in line with these morals and values and make a note as to how you feel.

The second area that integrity creates positive thoughts and attitudes is in our commitments to ourselves and others; being honest about the agreements we make. We tend to find it simple to keep our integrity with others, although there are plenty of individuals that even seem to struggle with that, but many of us never consider keeping our integrity with ourselves. Spencer Johnson put it this way, "Integrity is telling myself the truth. And honesty is telling the truth to other people." When was the last time you promised yourself that you would work out 3 times a week or wouldn't eat another piece of candy, only to find that your promise barely lasted a day? How often have you promised yourself that you would stay focused, in action and on task only to get distracted by tending your "farm" - a reference to the games on Facebook that encourage daily, even hourly participation to get the maximum scores in the game? Making these agreements and then not sticking to them means that you are not being honest with yourself. You are out of integrity.

When we cannot maintain integrity with ourselves, it creates self doubt. After all, you wouldn't continue to trust someone that repeatedly broke their promises to you therefore, you also start to not trust you with the promises you make to yourself. You begin to doubt your own words. Self doubt is negative energy and counterproductive to our desires to maintain our positive attitude. You lose confidence and feel lousy. You become convinced you won't be able to reach your goals. After all, nothing you have ever promised yourself came through so why would this be any different.

Integrity and the YOUniverse.

Not only have you let yourself down, you have also let down the YOUniverse. The YOUniverse really wants to provide for your requests. However, it won't give you what you can't handle. Let's say you want a new car worth $40,000 or a new home worth $350,000 or to make $250,000 a year. You set the intention, begin to visualize your goal as if it were already a part of your life and state your affirmations every day. But you get nowhere. You begin to doubt that any of this self help stuff works and wonder why you bothered to spend so much money on it in the first place.

In the midst of all those wonderful steps to achieve your goal, however, you missed the fact that you had promised yourself you'd start working out every day. You missed your agreement to eat healthy and not spend money on lattes each morning. What difference do those things make? The only one you let down was yourself, right?

When you set a big hairy audacious goal for yourself, the YOUniverse says, "You think so? You can't even stick to the little promises you make. You'll never achieve THAT goal!" With this kind of subconscious attitude, it is nearly impossible to just tell yourself that you can and believe it. It's a battle you aren't likely to win.

ACTION STEP

Start eliminating self doubt by creating goals that you KNOW you will stick to. Stretch a little but not too much. The idea here is to build confidence within yourself by reaching your goals.

For example, set a goal today, to exercise 30 minutes a day four times this week. That's it. Do not promise yourself that you will start working out every day or even every other day without an end to that promise. It must have a clear point in which you can measure that the commitment was a success.

Each time you reach one of your goals, celebrate and set another one. Work up a little bit each time. Set the goal to work out 30 minutes four times a week for two weeks or 45 minutes four times a week.

Continue to set manageable goals with a clearly defined outcome until you can look back and have a great deal of integrity and self confidence for all the things you can accomplish!

Do this with everything you promise yourself. Don't make promises you can't or won't keep. It makes all the difference in the world.

Remember, it takes practice.

18

ADOPT A PERSONAL MANTRA

Mantras or slogans are things that we can say to ourselves to remind us to focus on the positive. Literally, a mantra is a sound, word or series of words capable of creating a change. It has become very common for people to wear little rubber bracelets with phrases or slogans reminding them of their favorite thought. Having this reminder is a great idea whether it is a bracelet, a note card in your pocket or a message on your voicemail. Refer to your mantra when you are starting to feel the negative thoughts welling up. Remind yourself of why you chose this particular mantra in the first place and the benefits you will have with maintaining a more positive attitude.

If you aren't sure of what a mantra is, here are a few examples. You have probably heard many of these before.

"Put on your big girl panties and deal with it."

"Just Do It."

"Git'er Done!"

"Never let defeat rob you of success."

"Ask yourself, 'will this be important to me when I am 80 years old?'"

"Tomorrow is another day."

"The sun will come out tomorrow."

"The darkness of the midnight will not remain forever. Have a trust that the sunshine is on its way."

"Act as if it were impossible to fail."

"What would Jesus do?"

"Live Strong"

These are all very good personal mantras and have been used successfully by a number of individuals, however, the best one is one that you create or choose for yourself.

My mantra changes with time. When I first created one, it was a simple, "Be Present". This was a clear reminder to myself that only right now was important and tomorrow wasn't worth worrying about.

ACTION STEP

Choose or create a mantra that feels right to you. One that puts you in a positive frame of mind just by saying or thinking it. You can use one of the ones included above or create your own. It should be short and memorable but have meaning to you.

Once you have created your mantra, write it down and keep it with you at all times until you are able to recite it on a whim when it is most needed.

Your mantra, like mine, may change over time. It is a living thing that should be able to grow and transform just as you are growing.

Remember, it takes practice.

19

YOUR DAILY SHOWER

"People often say that motivation doesn't last. Well, neither does bathing - that's why we recommend it daily."

— Zig Ziglar

There is a lot of discussion on the topic of using daily motivation to shift a negative attitude to a positive one. Some people think that, since motivation doesn't last, it shouldn't be a valid technique for attitude adjustment. While it may not be a permanent shift, motivation can be a valuable and necessary band aid until the wound is healed. After using the tips, tools and techniques offered in the pages of this book, your attitude will naturally be more positive and inspiring. Despite that, we all face extra challenges in life that test our resolve to keep up that new positive attitude. At these times, having established a habit of daily motivation will be an important support tool.

ACTION STEP

Motivation can come in many forms. Find at least one that fits you well and do it daily. Then find two or three more that can be done weekly as an added boost. Here are some recommendations but you can be as creative as you like.

Read – This is my personal favorite. Every single day, I read something motivating and inspiring. The source may vary but I start each day with 20 minutes without fail. Personal development books or blogs, magazines such as *Success Magazine*, quotes or the Bible are all good choices.

Listen – Create a playlist or CD of your favorite inspirational songs. Some favorites might include the following.

- *It's My Life*, Bon Jovi
- *I'm Walking On Sunshine*, Katrina and the Waves
- *Break Free*, Shirley Levi

- *Man in Motion*, Night Ranger
- *My Way*, Paul Anka and Frank Sinatra
- *Believe it or Not*, from the TV series The Greatest American Hero
- *We are the Champions*, Queen
- *Free Will*, Rush

This list could go on and on. Take some time to put together your playlist of favorites. Search the internet for "songs that motivate and inspire" for more ideas.

Once you have your music ready, keep it handy to listen to when you need a boost or use it during workouts or drive time for regular inspiration.

Another option for listening is audio books and personal development programs on CD or MP3.

Watch – There is a plethora of movies available that can provide obvious or hidden lessons to life. Have one or two of them on hand to watch when your brain is ready to shut down and your focus is lost on anything else. Here are the ones I always go back to:

- *The Pursuit of Happyness*
- *The Ultimate Gift*
- *Facing the Giants*

- *Rudy* - or just about any sports related movie
- *Lean on Me*
- *What the Bleep Do We Know?*
- *Door to Door – The Story of Bill Porter*
- *Homeless to Harvard*

You can also find clips from these and other inspiring movies on sites such as Youtube.com.

Whether you read, listen or watch isn't as important as actually doing something daily. You may also find motivation through other means such as exercise or meditation. Each person will have their own unique combination. Find yours and do it.

Remember, it takes practice.

20

TAKE NOTE AND CELEBRATE

"Not taking time to celebrate your successes is like going to the amusement park and not riding any of the rides."

– Nicole Bandes

As young children, everything was worthy of celebrating. It might be something as simple as finding a pretty rock or as special as creating a work of art worthy of the fridge door. It didn't matter what it was, we wanted to share our excitement with everyone within our line of sight, especially our moms.

Maybe it was mom getting tired of all of our wonderful little successes that finally broke us of the celebration habit or maybe it was just that those little things didn't seem quite as worthy of celebration as the years went along. Whatever the reason, as adults, we tend to dismiss the moments in our lives that are worthy of celebrating. We might think that these moments aren't that special or that they weren't a big deal so why celebrate?

Taking note of our successes and finding a way to celebrate them reminds us that we can accomplish what we set out to do. It helps to build our self esteem and confidence level and encourages us to keep going. It gives us the ability to withstand some of the more challenging obstacles we may face. Some things are easier to achieve than others but all things are worthy of celebration just like when we were children.

On a physiological level, celebration releases good chemicals in our brains very much like a drug. It doesn't matter if you choose to celebrate via singing and dancing or buying something special or taking some extra time for yourself. The act of celebrating your success releases the feel good chemicals making you desire more success. You may even come to crave it and seek it out just for the feelings you get from it.

ACTION STEP

Begin keeping a journal of all of your successes. Be generous with yourself in what counts as a success as you have probably already spent too many years being stingy.

As you record your successes, start to formulate your celebration program. Try out some of these ideas for celebrating:

- Dance
- Sing
- Jump up and down wildly shouting "HURRAY!"
- Listen to a favorite song such as *Celebration* by Kool and the Gang or *Tonight's Gonna Be a Good Night* by Black Eyed Peas
- Buy something amazing
- Make a chart and put a gold star on it
- Find something completely original to yourself.

No matter which way you choose to celebrate, it helps if you can find a way to share it with others and allow them to help you celebrate. Find a celebration partner or use social media sites such as Facebook to post your successes and enjoy the number of congratulations and likes you get.

Keep your journal up to date to use during times when you struggle to feel positive. Let it serve as a reminder of all the wonderful things you are doing on a regular basis.

Remember, it takes practice.

21

A FEW MORE

It's all about over-delivering. Here are a few bonus tips for a more positive attitude:

Find your Passion – It is hard to have a positive attitude if we hate what we are doing. There are many successful people that are miserable because, while they have a lot of money, fame, or stuff, they aren't doing what has meaning in their lives. You may not be able to make the leap from what you are currently doing to what your purpose is, but you can usually find ways to include some of it in your spare time.

Change What You Watch and/or Read – Quite often the source of our entertainment leads to a negative attitude. Do you tend to watch reality tv or read magazines about the latest escapades of this actor or that actress? These types of entertainment tend to be full of negativity which perpetuates our own negativity. Instead, choose to read biographies of successful people, personal development books or the Bible. Find programming that is full of inspiration or at least neutral. Or stop watching TV altogether.

Laugh a Little – Or a Lot! Find sources of humor and utilize them at times when the negative attitude is prevailing. But be careful to avoid the types of humor that perpetuate negative thoughts. Although this humor can be very funny, it doesn't help us to turn our focus away from negative thinking.

Exercise – As much as we may not like to move our bodies, exercise has been proven to increase the feel good chemicals in our brain and make it easier to think positive. Take a walk, dance, play with your kids: it doesn't matter what you do, just that you do something physical.

Release Control – There are many things in life that we can't control. The only thing we can control at all times in all situations is our own reactions. Give up the need to control things you can't. It's very freeing.

Do Something Different – You've spent years doing what you have been doing and nothing has changed for you. Do something radically different.

Change your Questions – Instead of Why questions, start asking How questions. Why focuses on the past and present whereas How focuses on the future. For example, "Why am I not finding a better job?" can be rephrased, "How can I find a better job?" You don't need to be able to answer the question, you simply need to put it out there and be open to receiving the answer when it comes.

Have FUN! – I'm still amazed at how many of my coaching clients forget to have fun. Take time to be a kid again, to laugh and play.

Learn From the Experience of Others - Read about and observe how other people have come back from even worse adversity than you are now experiencing. Rags-to-riches stories, overcoming tremendous odds, persevering through failure. If they can do it, so can you.

Make Personal Growth a Lifelong Hobby – The more you grow, the easier it is to be a positive thinker.

And, remember, it takes practice.

22

TAKE ACTION NOW!

"If it is to be, it's up to me!"

\- Unknown

The only way to make anything within this book work for you and create the lasting change that you are desperately seeking is to take immediate action. You have made it this far already so don't let the end of the book make you think the work is over. On the contrary, it has just begun. Knowledge without action is like a car without gas, nice to look at but it won't get you anywhere. So fill up the car and take it out for a spin!

If you haven't already, go back through each chapter and take your time to integrate each technique into your daily life. Practice, practice, practice until it becomes habit. Then move on to the next chapter. You do not need to do the chapters in order. Find your favorites first and work through those. Once you have one technique mastered, then pick another one. I encourage you to give each and every chapter your best effort.

The Best Piece of Advice Ever Given

If you struggle with a certain technique, utilize the best piece of advice ever given. Want to know what it is? It's a doozie. Are you sure you are ready because this alone will change your life.

Ask for help.

That's it. It comes down to those 3 little words but is so all encompassing that it works in all cases at all times.

- When you are unsure what to do, ask for help.
- When you want the sale, ask for help.
- When you want a raise, ask for help.

- When you are afraid, ask for help.

- When you are worried, ask for help.

- When you have a problem, ask for help.

- When you have a solution, ask for help.

In many of the personal coaching programs, self help seminars and personal development books I have read, they offer this piece of advice in various ways.

- Find a mentor.

- Seek out the top people in your profession and ask what their best advice is.

- Hire a coach.

- Get support from those around you.

- Lean on someone else.

- Share your goals with others.

All of these say the same thing: Ask for help. It sure seems like pretty good advice to me!

Now it is easy to tell someone to go ask for help. It sounds great in theory. However, it isn't always easy for many of us, just as it wasn't easy for me when I started. In fact, I think one of my biggest life breakthroughs was when I finally stepped outside of my own comfort zone and asked for help. It was both the hardest and the best thing I ever did. It is about as close to the dividing line between before and after as there is in my life.

But how did I do it? For me it was a matter of finally getting so tired of not being able to figure it out on my own that asking for help was my last resort. If I didn't, it meant failure and failure meant going back to work a regular job which I knew would just about kill me, therefore, that failure was not an option.

You don't have to wait to get to that point though. Start small. Ask for little things for which you aren't attached to the outcome. Ask a stranger for a piece of gum or directions. Ask your spouse to get you something he or she wouldn't normally get you. Ask your children NOT to make their bed today. If you get what you are asking for, great. If not, no big deal. Make it a practice, a game, to ask for things and see how people respond. As you build up an ability to ask and receive or ask and not, but not feel rejected or ashamed, you will be able to ask for bigger, more important things.

Start to notice that you ask for things all day long, every day. You ask for coffee at the coffee shop, and probably ask for them to make it exactly the way you like it. You ask to merge into traffic when you turn your signal on. You ask to have someone take your phone call or meet you for an appointment.

We can't exist on our own. We can't possibly provide 100% of all of our own needs. Even a hermit in the woods has items in his possession for which he is not responsible for creating himself. Other people are there to help us but it is up to us to let them know what our needs are.

"But I prefer to give. I'm not a good receiver. "

Then give the gift of allowing someone to help you. Most people are generally givers. They like to help other people when they can. It makes them feel good to help. Don't deprive them of that gift by not asking for help. Would you feel bad if you could do something for someone and they didn't ask you for help? You probably would. Most people would. Don't make someone else feel bad because they can help you but you are too afraid to ask.

So go out and hire a coach or seek out a mentor. Asking others for help can be one of our biggest challenges to overcome but will also be one of the most rewarding.

Anyone can *Have* a *Nice* day,

choose to **MAKE** yours **AMAZING!**

SPECIAL OFFER

YOU COACHING FREE ASSESSMENT

Because we understand that it is sometimes a challenge to apply what you have learned in a book to your own personal situation, and because one of the best pieces of advice ever given is to ask for help, we would like to make a special offer to those individuals that have taken the step towards their own positivity by purchasing this book. Golden Eagles Coaching is offering you one free YOU Coaching assessment. In this 30 minute assessment, you will learn about YOU Coaching, how it can help YOU to overcome your own negative thinking and make a lasting shift that will help to create more abundance, wealth and happiness in your life. In addition, YOU will go away with at least one insight that will begin to create the positive change immediately.

To request your free assessment,
visit www.goldeneaglescoaching.com/contact/ and enter
POP Offer in the subject line.

This offer is subject to availability with one of our YOU Coaches. There is a limit of one offer per copy of *Positivity on Purpose* purchased. While the value of this assessment is set at $65, the offer cannot be redeemed for cash. Additional fees and charges may apply at the time of scheduling.

Notes

1. Jorge Moll, Frank Krueger,Roland Zahn, Matteo Pardini, Ricardo de Oliveira-Souza, and Jordan Grafman (2006). Human fronto–mesolimbic networks guide decisions about charitable donation [Abstract]. http://www.pnas.org/content/103/42/15623.abstract

2. Values assessment tool - http://www.ethicalleadership.org/Self%20Guided%20Core%2 0Values%20Exercise.pdf

Thanks to Ross Murker, who helped with editing. Ross helps people fuel their life, health, and prosperity: http://rwmurker.bodybyvi.com

ABOUT THE AUTHOR

Nicole Bandes has a degree in Psychology from Northern Arizona University. Her honors include President of Psi Chi (National Honor Society for Psychology) and graduating Magna Cum Laude.

Nicole began her journey over 30 years ago when, as a young child, she decided she wanted to own her own business. Coming from a working parent background where the belief was to get a good job and work till you retire (if lucky), this was a little unusual.

Nicole has spent several years attempting to discover who she was and why she was here. She always knew she was meant for greater things than what she was doing. Nicole struggled with self esteem, confidence and direction in her life. But, through many years of self discovery, education and personal development she has found her path and now she wants to help others find theirs.

In 2010, Nicole created YOU Coaching, a unique combination of life and professional coaching that creates positive change for ultimate success. To find out more about how you can work with Nicole for coaching or to hire her as a trainer at your next event, visit

www.GoldenEaglesCoaching.com.